Chesham
In Living Memory

Peter Hawkes & Phil Cox

Dedication

This book is dedicated to **R F East** *(right)* and **A J Scrivener** *(below)*.

Ray East was born in Chesham in 1927. He spent most of his working life as a skilled motor garage mechanic. On retirement, Ray decided to record his home town in photographs. As an early member of Chesham Camera Club, he pursued a keen interest in black-and-white photography, processing and printing. He also spent many years collecting and archiving old photographs which he copied from his many contacts in Chesham. Ray was often seen about town with bicycle and camera until failing eyesight limited his hobby. To witness the publication of much of his collection was a long-term ambition fulfilled. Ray died in 2015.

Joe Scrivener was an Associate of the Royal Photographic Society and the founder of Chesham Camera Club in 1963. He joined forces with members of Amersham Photographic Club, including Stan Flello, Les Slatter, Len Bristow, Matt Chapel and Eddie Brown, to create the new group. Joe was the Club's first chairman and later served for many years as president. He made an extensive photographic record of Chesham during the 1960s and '70s and gifted many of his prints to Ray East. A shield is still awarded at the Chesham Photographic Club in Joe Scrivener's name, as well as a trophy donated by his wife, Irene. Joe died during the 1980s.

Chesham Photographic Club

In 2009 the Camera Club changed its name to Chesham Photographic Club, to more accurately reflect its aims. It continues to provide friendly and informative meetings for anyone interested in photography. Its programme includes talks, competitions, workshops, and audio-visual presentations and is based at the White Hill Centre. **www.cheshamphotoclub.co.uk**

Photographic sources

The majority of the photographs published within this book are from the Ray East Collection. Every effort has been made to seek copyright permission for the reproduction of photos. Any omissions are entirely unintentional and we apologise to any copyright holders who have not been consulted. Any such omissions will be corrected in future editions. The very early images are likely to have been made by two prominent photographers of the time, William Butts and William Coles. During the 20th century, many images of the town were made by Graham Shelton, Sydney Jowett, Edwin & Walter East, Stan Cox and Hector Smith, as well as the photographers of the *Bucks Examiner* and the *Middlesex County Press*. Recent photographic acknowledgements can be found on page 51.

First published in 2016 by Hawkes Design & Publishing Ltd

Peter Hawkes and Phil Cox have asserted their moral rights to be identified as the authors of this work.

ISBN: 978-0-9554707-7-6

ABOVE: *Photographer and collector, Ray East, with camera and bicycle, in Market Square.*

Contents

ABOVE: Ray East photographing the clock tower under construction in Market Square, 1992.

Other publications from Hawkes Design & Publishing Ltd 01494 793000 www.hawkesdesign.co.uk

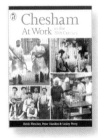

Chesham at Work in the 20th Century
by Keith Fletcher, Peter Hawkes and Lesley Perry
A history of the main sectors of trade and manufacture that provided work and a livelihood for Chesham people through the 20th century. A celebration of Chesham's industrial heritage, and a portrait of its workers and the many varied items that they produced in the town. **£12.95 inc p&p**

Pubs & Inns of Chesham & Villages
by Ray East, Keith Fletcher and Peter Hawkes
A fascinating guide to the historic public houses of Chesham and district, including more than twenty establishments that are still serving today. Featuring over 100 alehouses, inns, taverns and beer shops in the town centre and the surrounding Buckinghamshire villages.
£12.95 inc p&p CURRENTLY SOLD OUT & AWAITING REPRINT

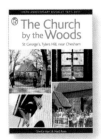

The Church by the Woods
by Sheila Hart and Neil Rees
For the first time, the story of St George's Church, Tylers Hill - its building and congregation – is brought to life by newspaper reports, Miss Bangay's memoirs and the memories of villagers, vicars and veterans of its many organisations and groups. This booklet is richly illustrated with about 100 beautiful photographs from then and now. **£7.50 inc p&p**

Holmer Green Heroes of WW1
by Stuart King & Chris Peers
Remembering those who died in the First World War in this Buckinghamshire village.
Due for publication 2016

Faith in Chesham & Villages
by Colin Cartwright, Neil Rees and Peter Hawkes
A history of church and chapel folk in and around Chesham over 1,000 years. **This long awaited book is due out 2017**

Chairmaker's Cottage to Chiltern Chapel
by Betty Twitchen and Neil Rees
Over 200 years in the history of a Buckinghamshire village – Lane End, near High Wycombe. **£7 inc. p&p**
CURRENTLY SOLD OUT

Why look back at the past?

PICTURED: The three larger photographs on this two page spread are all taken at roughly the same point in Chesham High Street, adjacent to Francis Yard, over a period of 100 years.

There is little point in longing for the past – it has gone – and despite our perception of things having sometimes been better back then, time has most certainly moved on. It makes far more sense to live in the present moment and to accept, as best as possible, the way life is right now. Nevertheless, it is useful to look back at the past in order to understand how we've arrived at where we are today. It is particularly important, in planning for the future, to value the skills, wisdom and cultural heritage passed down to us by those who came before and, sometimes, to learn from their mistakes!

When photography was invented in the first half of the 19th century, the use of cameras allowed people to vividly capture Chesham's townscapes, people and historical events. We have evidence of these images from about 1880. Change is life's only constant. However, despite almost everything having been demolished and replaced in this town centre view of that time, it is still very much recognisable as Chesham Broadway.

Having published old pictures on social media, especially on the *Chesham Heritage* facebook site, we received substantially more responses and feedback to photographs within living memory, in particular from the 1960s onwards. The evolving design of cars caught people's attention, as did changing shop fronts and meeting places. There was inevitably a disappointment at the short-sightedness of the planners of that time, who swept away many much-valued buildings and landmarks, without respect for the past and with an unrealistic vision of the future. Thankfully, we live in times where a greater balance has been achieved between architectural heritage and technological advancement.

How Chesham has changed!

What was Chesham like in 1900? No one is alive who remembers. We can see from old photographs, like the fascinating one at the top of the page opposite, that the roads were unsurfaced and rutted by cart wheels. Horses were the main mode of transport, along with bicycles and steam trains which had arrived in Chesham by the 1890s. The petrol engine had been invented in Germany in 1885, but in Great Britain the Locomotive Act had put severe limitations on mechanically propelled vehicles driven on the roads. It was another ten years before this Act was abolished, giving the green light for the age of the motor car and for great changes to our town.

Mr Cheeld, an engineer, was the first person to own a motor car in Chesham. A wealthy or sporting background were other likely qualifications for early motoring enthusiasts, as journeys required careful planning and technical abilities. There were no petrol stations for refuelling or motor garages in the case of breakdown. The first garages to cater for these new vehicles were often established by those who were already trading as cycle dealers, coachbuilders or ironmongers.

By 1939 there were over two million vehicles on Britain's roads, but the war effort and the austere years that followed kept things in check. Few people could have predicted the impact that cars would have on the town centre in the decades that followed.

ABOVE: *Mr Cheeld built Chesham's first motor car at Lord's Mill between 1900 and 1902. It was called 'Emma' and apparently still does the London to Brighton run.*

Architectural conservation in Chesham

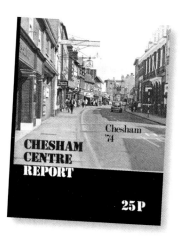

TOP: Val Biro's illustration of his famous 1929 Austin car 'Gumdrop,' drawn for a Chesham publication.

CHESHAM CENTRE REPORT

Chesham '74

25P

ABOVE:
A booklet issued in 1974, which drew on Colin Buchanan's book 'Traffic in Towns' in proposing a planning solution to Chesham's traffic congestion dilemma.

BELOW:
Perhaps the most tragic and unnecessary architectural losses suffered by Chesham town: the 15th century Crown coaching inn and 17th century Town Hall in Market Square, the ancient Lord's Mill at Waterside and the 1937 art deco Embassy cinema in Germain Street.

The Chesham Society

Founded in 1957, the Chesham Society was originally described in the local newspaper as 'a preservationist body, established to protect the old and picturesque parts of town'. This was not an unfair label, considering the need to challenge the general post-war trend towards bulldozing any old and decaying buildings, to welcome in a brave new age of modernism. The Society's first issue was opposing the proposed widening of Church Street, and saving from demolition some of the town's oldest domestic dwellings, including no.54, dating from the 14th century. Despite a positive outcome in this case, the Society had a particularly tough job in those early years, with prior access to any development plans blocked by the authorities. Society members were prepared to 'fight to the death' to keep the 17th century Town Hall in Market Square. Equally determined, but intent on pulling it down, were members of the Chesham Chamber of Trade and Commerce. Three quarters of the town's traders wanted it demolished, and they got their way.

One of the founders of the Chesham Society was Val Biro. He moved to the town in 1954 and illustrated a booklet, *Discovering Chesham*. He was Hungarian born, and a great believer in parochial life. It took an outsider to see the bigger picture and recognise Chesham's value. Val wrote "We must retain that peculiar characteristic which makes up the town. We could lose it all and gain nothing".

Without the voice of Val Biro and the many valuable members of the Society over the years, the town could have lost so much more. Just one example is the retention of the complete west side of Market Square and the Golden Ball public house, which the planners had intended to flatten in the construction of St Mary's Way. A great many years were also spent by the Society campaigning against a proposed link road, destined to funnel four lanes of traffic from Old Amersham, across the fields to the west, and directly into Chesham. This disastrous proposal was successfully defeated.

Since the 1990s, traffic issues have diminished and the Chesham Society's main aim these days is to promote the highest standards in planning, design, building and restoration appropriate to the town and its people; also to protect and enhance the built and natural heritage of Chesham; to maintain and improve the environment and amenities enjoyed by local people and visitors; and to encourage public interest in the history and character of the town and its continuing care. Find out more at **www.cheshamsociety.org.uk**

During the compilation of this book, the author found *The History of the Chesham Society – A Personal View*, written by Jennifer Moss, to be invaluable in providing an accurate timeframe for the recent changes to the townscape. In this substantial work, Jennifer concludes: "Since the 1950s and 1960s there has been a sea change in public appreciation of the value of old buildings. Then, old buildings in a poor state of repair would have been swept away without a thought, in the interests of 'modernisation'. Now they are lovingly restored and much valued and Church Street today illustrates this well". Coincidentally, it was a resident of the old town who collected many historical articles from the *Bucks Examiner* during the decades of radical change. The scrapbooks of M Narraway, who lived at 108 Church Street, also made fascinating and very useful reading.

St Mary's Way and East Street

Early mention must be made of St Mary's Way, as it had such a profound effect on the town's other highways mentioned in the following chapters. The main photograph above gives a good indication of the main High Street running horizontally through the middle of the valley, with East Street at the top and St Mary's Way below. This image, taken in 1989, shows one way traffic filling the High Street, heading south towards Red Lion Street, while northbound traffic snakes through Market Square to go north towards Broad Street. The open scar in the right-hand corner is a result of work in progress to re-route traffic away from Market Square and to widen St Mary's Way for two-way traffic, thus allowing High Street pedestrianisation.

Relief for the traffic-congested High Street was long sought after. East Street was constructed in 1966 as a service road to allow shop deliveries from the rear where possible. It cut through several yards and back gardens, running alongside the old bowling green. St Mary's Way was proposed as a relief road in 1965. The first stage, completed in 1968, incorporated a pedestrian subway *(pictured under construction, top left)*. The final stage came two decades later. The four-lane carriageway is now screened by a long brick wall *(replacing the temporary picket fence shown top right)*.

BELOW: An hour glass graphic, from the 1974 'Chesham Centre Report,' illustrating the narrow valley bottom between the steep fields of Dungrove and the 36-acre Lowndes Park, with its Skottowes pond. This helps explain the tight restrictions on road widths.

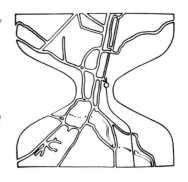

9

Red Lion Street

The first road scheme and rebuilding to cater for new motor traffic took place at Red Lion Corner in the late 1930s. Here stood the original Red Lion Inn *(above)*, built in 1723 to provide stabling and refreshment on the road to London. The highway at this point had been navigable by horses and carts, but buses and lorries often became wedged in the bottle neck when they failed to give way.

The Red Lion, and another inn a few doors along, The Nag's Head, were demolished along with the cottages and yard in between. A new pub was built behind the existing Red Lion, prior to its demolition in 1937. Red Lion Street was then opened up to busy traffic, as it headed towards Waterside and the Amersham Road. The contrast in the resulting view and road width can be seen from the main photographs above and below, taken from roughly the same point.

ABOVE: An Amersham & District bus squeezes through Red Lion Corner in 1932.

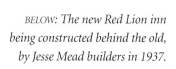

BELOW: The new Red Lion inn being constructed behind the old, by Jesse Mead builders in 1937.

TOP: *Another pre-1937 view of Red Lion Corner from the opposite direction, as seen when travelling from the Amersham Road towards Market Square. To the right of Baldwin's shop and its street signs was the entrance to Stratford's Yard and Townfield Yard.*

LEFT: The same street view in 1972. Here there is a left turn into Germain Street, or onwards through Market Square to the relatively new St Mary's Way. First right is East Street, a service road built in 1966 that cut through many of the Yards behind the High Street.

BELOW: Mayo & Hawkes cycle shop began in a small cottage in Red Lion Street. This was demolished in 1958 and rebuilt in the architecture of the time. It was the first shop in Chesham to have a large plate glass window and is a good example of the bold and functional, yet incongruous designs that appeared in the name of modernisation.

The Broadway

Chesham Broadway, once known as Pillory Green, is the centre of the modern town. Centuries-old texts describe gatherings in the large open space beside 'the great elm'. Here there were fairs, celebrations, announcements and remembrances.

As more people began to buy their own motor cars in the early decades of the 20th century, it became increasingly difficult to park directly outside the shop, church or public house of choice. Not surprisingly, therefore, the Broadway became the town's first car park. Parking bays were marked out with white lines by the war memorial, in front of Brandon's furnishing store, and further spaces were available in a layby opposite The Lamb public house, as pictured above in 1935.

Traffic could enter from north or south via the two-way High Street, or by Blucher Street from Bellingdon or Chartridge, and it could access the railway by Station Road. This side street had been built in the late 1880s by demolishing several houses in a section of the High Street.

By the 1940s the Broadway was proving to be inadequate for the town's parking requirements, and so plans were made for a larger space at Star Yard and, later in the same decade, an extended war memorial and garden were designed to commemorate another major world conflict.

PICTURED: A horse sale in the Broadway in 1914. The last fair to be held was in 1937, before transferring to the Moor, but the carousel returns every Christmas to continue the tradition.

PICTURED: *Various motor vehicles gathered in the Broadway.*

In front of the Broadway Baptist Church about 1910 (top). The early motorist would usually have had wealth, technical ability and sporting instincts! When the vehicle broke down, he or his chauffeur had to repair it.

Between the white lined bays in front of Brandon's (middle) stand British makes such as Morris, Humber and Austin, in the 1920s.

Outside Goss's tea rooms in 1936 stand several cars (left) ready for an outing organised by traders after early closing on a Thursday.

TOP: By the 1960s and '70s, most highways were not only cluttered with vehicles, but also with direction signs, road markings and 'street furniture': zebra crossings, belisha beacons, kerbs, bollards, municipal street lights and bus stops – all ready for young people to tick off in their 'I-Spy On a Car Journey' books!

RIGHT & BELOW: This stretch of the Broadway, where it combines with the busy High Street, is now less easy to recognise. Following the demolition of the House of Tree and Goss's café in 1968, the buildings to the right of this main image, and also the Lamb public house, with its pargetted frontage, came down in 1974, despite much protest from the Chesham Society. They were replaced by the nondescript buildings where Boot's the Chemist and Waterstones bookshop currently trade.

The Broadway has served as a bus terminus for many decades. A roundabout system was set up in 1963, centred on the war memorial, but through-traffic is currently restricted, with buses and taxis taking priority. The imposing store of Brandon & Sons furnishers replaced a curve of very old, picturesque cottages in the 1920s. Sixty years later, a brash red and yellow shop sign indicated the latest newcomer – Derek Cousins' discount store. These days, the building is divided up into several tasteful retail units. Across the road, the Eastern Electricity shop occupied the old premises of Webb's brushmakers. Since then it has been attractively refurbished as Caffè Nero.

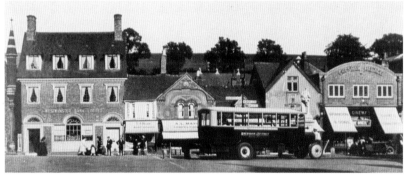

PICTURED: In the 1920s, these open top charabancs were used for outings, especially to the seaside and to sporting events. The first motor buses offering greater comfort appeared shortly after, such as this Amersham & District model. Many rival firms operated through Chesham Broadway, including Green Line, Rover and Lee & District. Gilberts Taxis has also operated from here since 1956. The Chesham Palace cinema, later renamed The Astoria, closed in 1959 and was demolished in the 1970s. The glass-fronted replacement building was initially used by the Co-operative Society and is currently a branch of the Superdrug store.

Blucher Street

The photographs on this page show Blucher Street leading away from the Broadway, chosen to aid identification of this corner of town, now almost totally obliterated. Named after General Blucher, this road with its terraced cottages was known as Bridge Street or Bury Hill End prior to the Battle of Waterloo. To the left, beyond the decorated arch *pictured above* by the Broadway Baptist Church is The Star Inn, demolished in 1938 along with the adjoining yard and fourteen small cottages behind, to create the town's first major car park. Star Yard remains the largest area of parking in town.

BELOW LEFT: Blucher Street seen in the distance, viewed from Chesham Broadway in the 1960s.

BELOW RIGHT: A closer view, with one side of the street already demolished.

The opposite side of the street was demolished in the 1950s to create further car parking, with the exception of two shops by the Broadway; then the remainder of the street was lost to St Mary's Way roundabout. The town gained a library and the first Elgiva theatre, built in Elgiva Lane in the 1970s.

ABOVE: The Broadway Baptist Church is on the Star Yard side of Blucher Street. This terrace once had three pubs within its length. The row of cottages was fully demolished in 1968. The opposite side of the street has already been flattened in this photograph.

LEFT: Almost all of Blucher Street is now swept away for car parking, roundabout and St Mary's Way. The white gabled buildings are all that remain.

BELOW: The current Chesham Library was built in 1970 on the site of these attractive cottages and their front gardens on the north side of Blucher Street.

RIGHT: Where once The Blue Ball inn served Benskin's beer, now stands this roundabout, dividing four lanes of traffic as it thunders along the town's relief road, allowing the pedestrianised High Street and attractive Lowndes Park to act as healthy lungs for the town.

Avenue House, on the corner, has now also gone as, of course, has the great avenue of elm trees across the park, felled in 1950, before this photograph was taken. Proposals to plant a new avenue of trees have, to date, regrettably not been successful.

BELOW: This is all that remains of Blucher Street. Climpson's sold wine and spirits until closure in the mid-1970s, after which the building was threatened with demolition. Thankfully, a timber-framed 17th century gatehouse was revealed and restored. It now leads through to an attractive cobbled courtyard with small shop premises, one currently selling handmade chocolates!

Market Square

A Market Hall was first recorded in 1679 and it would have been used as a corn exchange, where grain could be kept dry. The building was enlarged by Lord Chesham in 1856. The lower storey was an open piazza, although later enclosed, and the upper storey was used as a Town Hall for court and council sessions. It was also used for theatre and cinema.

By the early 1960s the Town Hall was storm damaged and falling into disrepair. The clock tower was removed and the building boarded up. The High Street was becoming increasingly busy with cars, and plans had long been discussed to create a relief road. Market Square was seen as part of the solution. Tragically, there was only limited opposition to the demolition of this 17th century landmark and it was finally removed in 1965.

ABOVE: An illustration made in 1960 by the Chesham Society, depicting its vision of how the Town Hall could be opened up again, making it less dark and sombre. Further drawings were made of a reduced and revised structure, but the demolition team made swift work of the building's removal just a few years later.

With the removal of the Market Hall, the way was clear for the construction of St Mary's Way. Northbound traffic would be allowed through the Market Square and round the sharp corner to the relief road, while southbound traffic could continue down the High Street. From 1968, and for two decades after, Market Square was a dual carriageway! Traffic also entered directly from Germain Street, making a zebra crossing and traffic island necessary for the safety of pedestrians.

RIGHT: Chesham Automatics serviced and sold fruit machines, video gaming and pinball machines, as well as providing juke boxes to pubs and cafés. They also began video hire on VHS and Betamax formats. Next door, to the left, Wright's corn and seed merchants is fondly remembered and the 16th century building has now been fully restored and is currently occupied by Frost's estate agents.

In 1989 plans were nearing completion to pedestrianise the High Street and Market Square. To free the town centre from through traffic, it was necessary to widen St Mary's Way, making it two lanes in both directions. Two buildings had to be demolished to allow traffic to bypass the Square. These had held two butcher's shops – Gomm's (later Archer's) and Derrick's (later Chesham Automatics) – the two buildings in the centre of the view *above*. The photograph *below* shows the extension of Red Lion Street in their place. Chesham also lost Chequers Yard in the process. The site of the old Chequers Inn was occupied from 1950 by Chesham Building Society *(pictured far right)*, which before its closure was known as the oldest building society in the world. The two demolished buildings are held at Chiltern Open Air Museum and will hopefully one day be reconstructed on their site. Market Square was fully pedestrianised by 1992.

RIGHT: W Brazil & Co, butchers, was established in the late 19th century, and moved its shop from Red Lion Street to Market Square about 1930. It closed in 1998, but the beautiful signage and tiling has been retained in a café setting. Outdoor seating is now being encouraged in Market Square.

Next door was the Crown Inn, dating from the 15th century. It was a coaching inn with galleried courtyard and was used as a local headquarters for Parliamentary forces during the Civil War of 1642. In more recent times it incorporated the Victoria Rooms, where meetings and dances took place.

The Crown was another tragic loss to the period of modernisation – demolished in 1957/8 and replaced by a small supermarket, occupied over the years by Fine Fare, Tesco, Bejam, Iceland and Circle7. The new building was set back three feet – an indication of the proposed widening of the High Street, which thankfully was not progressed.

BELOW: Chapter One bookshop was run by Liz Payne, who hosted many local book signings. In 1995 the late local historian George Piggin's new book was launched by the then Town Mayor, Derek Lacey, who had also been well known as a Chesham market trader.

The clock tower, the market and the museum

A new clock tower was built in 1992, featuring the original town clock. The fortunes of the market have much improved in recent years. The traditional Wednesday market, first granted in 1257, had died out in the early 1960s. In 1976 it was re-established, along with a Saturday market, in the Embassy cinema car park, with an official opening by *Coronation Street* actor William Roache (Ken Barlow!). In 1977 the host site was transferred to Albany Place car park, alongside St Mary's Way. Following pedestrianisation, Chesham market now uses the length of the High Street, with additional events, such as Local Produce and Art & Craft markets, held in the Market Square.

In 2009 Chesham Museum moved to Market Square and used the clock face design in its new logo. It took over the premises of Chapter One bookshop, having moved from the stable block of the Gamekeeper's Lodge in Bellingdon Road, where it had been established in 2004 by landlord Shay Comaskey along with Mora Walker, a stalwart member of the old Chesham Town Museum Project.

LEFT: Andrew Ketteringham and Arnold Baines, representing Chesham Town Council, are shown here by the clock tower foundation work.

The original Town Hall clock of 1856 was returned to Market Square in 1992 by Smith of Derby, clockmakers, whose experts also installed the mechanism.

In 2014 the original town bell, dating from 1748, was also reinstated in the clock tower after a campaign led by Stirling Maguire. A ceremony was held that year during which the bell was rung once for each Chesham soldier who died in the Great War.

Church Street

ABOVE: Note the Golden Ball pub's sign post just above the figures on the right in this photograph and compare its situation in the colour photograph on the page opposite, to realise just how much of this scene has now been flattened.

The Golden Ball pub itself (tucked out of sight) closed in 1985, but the building remains, currently converted to offices. The Chesham Society campaigned to protect it from the bulldozers, as plans for St Mary's Way had initially proposed its demolition.

RIGHT: In 1965, with the old Town Hall gone, this stretch of Church Street was due to be opened up to through traffic and was under further threat from the Highways Authority. In 1973, Colin Amery, Features Editor of 'The Architects Journal' wrote of Church Street: "One of the nicest streets I have seen. I am amazed that anyone could ever have thought of destroying any part of it".

Church Street is well conserved and little changed along much of its length, but the beginning of the street shown above, where it once linked with Market Square, has mostly been demolished. On the far left of the scene *above* is the corner of the old Town Hall. The very old building roughly in the centre of the Victorian photograph was removed in 1937, and the empty space was initially used for car parking. Three white gabled buildings remain on the left (numbers 4, 6 and 8) and at the time of publication are occupied by an art & craft shop and a café. The corner building shown below (no.2 Church Street) was the subject of an intense battle between members of the Highways Authority – who disliked the sharp road corner – and the Chesham Society who wished to see the old building preserved, and Market Square kept intact. It was, disappointingly, demolished in 1968.

TOP: *Shown here is Church Street in the early 1960s, with only a small car park, which had replaced some older dwellings, as an indication of the disruption to come. On the right can be seen the rear of Barnes' motor works in Parsonage Lane. Barnes had originally built horse-drawn coaches, but had evolved his business to become a painter of motor bodies by 1911. The Council for the Preservation of Rural England tried to save this fine three-storey building in 1968, but failed. The threat was St Mary's Way, Chesham's relief road built in that year, which is seen dominating the foreground of the same view below.*

LEFT: *The northbound traffic of St Mary's Way initially passed through Market Square to create the two-lane carriageway shown here. In the late 1980s it was re-routed, to avoid Market Square, requiring the demolition of the buildings in the near left of this photograph.*

BELOW: *Despite a large stretch of Church Street being demolished, the entrance to the old town remains very attractive. The Chesham Society campaigned to protect the street from widening – the more recently built no.'s 91 to 99 give an indication of what the planners had in mind. The Temperance Hall (below) has, since 1983, been the home of the Little Theatre by the Park.*

Watermeadow

BELOW: Behind the White Owl café was the Embassy car park. This has now been built over, while the meadow behind Church Street and Town Bridge, pictured, is now under tarmac for yet more parking. Thankfully, the Donkeyland meadow survives, as the church and watermeadow are the root of Chesham's original Saxon name 'Ceasteleshamm'.

The White Owl café in Church Street was previously known as The Blinking Owl, as it had a carved wooden owl outside that blinked. When this stopped working it became better known as The Winking Owl or, even better, The Greasy Sparrow! It was the place to meet from the late 1950s through to the early '80s, especially for teenagers, tradesmen and groups of touring cyclists! Fondly remembered are the juke box, pinball machines, full breakfasts and cups of tea, after which the young customers might well have moved on to the Co-operative Record Shop, the Embassy Cinema or Nettie Trieber's teen fashion store. As can be seen in the contrasting views above, most of these terraced cottages were cleared for the final phase of St Mary's Way in 1989 and to create an access road to the Watermeadow car park. The bread oven from the original Darvell's bakery premises of 1838 was rescued and taken to Chiltern Open Air Museum, along with the building which had housed Barnes' Church Street coachworks, with its double-gated yard entrance. The White Owl is now home to a Chinese restaurant.

Germain Street

With the demolition of the old Red Lion inn *(pictured above)* for road widening in 1937, following the construction of the new public house behind it *(pictured below, left),* several dwellings and shops at the street corner were demolished. However, most of the attractive period cottages still remain along its length. The offices of the *Bucks Examiner,* managed at this site by Page & Thomas from 1906, have stood empty since 2009, when the latest management transferred to Uxbridge.

Under the editorship of Frank Hiddlestone, affectionately known as 'Spec', the *Bucks Examiner* flourished and had a circulation of 9,500 in 1954, the year of his retirement. In 1960, following the introduction of lithographic technology, it was the first weekly newspaper in the country to carry a full-colour page advert and full-colour news photograph. Another long-term editor was Tony White, who maintained the publication through its later years in Chesham. In more recent times, the paper began to lose favour with the townspeople, and in 1994 an alternative newsletter was established by the community, *Chesham Town Talk,* which ran for almost 20 years. A privately owned magazine, *Your Chesham,* currently acts as an additional voice for the town.

Town Bridge

BELOW RIGHT: Germain Street lies either side of Town Bridge. In 1968, the Chesham Society successfully opposed plans to use Town Bridge as an entrance to the proposed new car park at Watermeadow. This opposition was supported by the Chiltern Society, at that time a relatively new countryside preservation group, which considered that Watermeadow ought to be protected as a conservation area. Despite works to strengthen the bridge in 1974, this part of town by Water Lane remains an unspoilt corner.

ABOVE: *Miss Faithorne's fine house in Germain Street, opposite the Bucks Examiner offices, is pictured here for sale in 1936. A sign was put up advertising the coming of a 'Super Cinema'. The editor of the newspaper was soon to write of the loss of this old dwelling with its peaceful gardens, mourning the demise of the view from his office window. Radical change is rarely accepted easily.*

BELOW: *The white façade of the Embassy stands in stark contrast to the dark and decaying remains of Gooding's Forge in the 1960s. During the Second World War this was the site of a German bomb drop that killed the blacksmith's daughter.*

The Embassy Cinema was designed in art deco style by David Nye and opened in Germain Street in 1937. It was managed by Shipman & King, the same company who ran The Rex at Berkhamsted. There was an attractive entrance foyer, a café with chrome and glass partitioning, two curved staircases and a large auditorium with decorative acoustic panels, which seated well over one thousand people. Much use was made of red and green neon lighting.

Cinema had become the most popular form of entertainment, with a rapid turnover of films and a mass turnout on Saturdays. Sunday performances were allowed after 1947. The cinema became so successful that it was decided that Chesham's previous picture palace, The Astoria, should be closed down. The premises in the Broadway had functioned as a cinema since 1914 (on the site of the current Superdrug) and ceased operations in May 1959.

The rise of television from the late 1950s, followed by the introduction of video technology in the 1970s, led to a temporary decline in cinema going. By the early 1980s, the new owners of the Embassy, Thorn-EMI, were determined that there was no longer a demand for cinema in the town. There was, however, much protest at its closure, and a full house for the final film screening in 1982. Prior to demolition in 1983/4, the Museum of London acquired some of the seating, lighting and carpets, a tribute to the high regard in which the design of the cinema was held. There is little doubt, in hindsight, that the Embassy could have carried on its success in later years if the building had been saved.

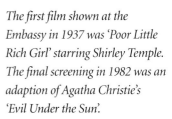

The first film shown at the Embassy in 1937 was 'Poor Little Rich Girl' starring Shirley Temple. The final screening in 1982 was an adaption of Agatha Christie's 'Evil Under the Sun'.

Such fond memories are recalled of Saturday morning 'flicks' during the 1950s, '60s and '70s. Going up the Embassy steps was reportedly like going into a palace, with the luxury carpet and seating. Younger children would get their bag of sweets from the corner shop by Town Bridge. Teenagers would prefer a coffee, with rock & roll tunes on the juke box, at the White Owl café in Church Street.

Nancy Hazlehurst ran the Embassy restaurant for many years. Ice creams and drinks were also sold in the auditorium during the break, while ushers stalked the aisles, puffing their cigarettes and searching with their torches for any misbehaviour!

Gilbert Marshall's adjoining car garage of the 1940s was later occupied by Chesham Furnishers. This showroom transferred to Bedworld in the High Street after the cinema was demolished, making way for the Town Bridge Court retirement flats (shown left).

High Street

BELOW: Chesham High Street in 1937, with the crowds and the traffic out to celebrate the Coronation of King George VI. The single union jack flag is above the entrance to Lacey's Yard.

In 1968, the town got a taste of pedestrianisation when the High Street shops closed for the day of Chesham United's trip to Wembley for the Amateur Cup Final. Despite being runners up in the end, the streets filled with the excited crowds.

A similar scene is still created in town every summer when the Chesham Carnival procession arrives; large crowds also gather at the end of each November for the Christmas shopping event.

Lower High Street

This narrow, serpentine route through the town is of ancient origin. Referring to the photograph above, the left-hand side of the street probably aligned with the old field boundary, while the right-hand side followed the path of a tributary of the River Chess, now culverted below the street. Once mostly residential, it evolved to become the town's centre of commerce, reaching a height of elegance and self-sufficiency between the world wars. Compared with Amersham, which is divided into an old town with a high standard of architectural preservation, and a new town on the hill built around the station, incorporating wide streets mostly laid out in the 1930s, Chesham had to accommodate an increasing flow of traffic in a relatively confined space, with narrow pavements and high levels of pollution making the High Street a hazardous thoroughfare by the 1960s.

CHESHAM UNITED
CUP FINAL
SOUVENIR

1967-68

TWO SHILLINGS AND SIXPENCE

PICTURED: *Three contrasting views of the same stretch of the Lower High Street, where it meets Market Square.*

The first is from 1912, showing the contruction of the Queen Anne style bank building. The unmetalled street leads away from the Town Hall in Market Square in the days when horses and carts were still the main means of transport.

The second is of the two-way street under tarmac shortly after the demolition of the Town Hall in 1965, for the benefit of motorised traffic. The National Provincial Bank, left, merged into the National Westminster in 1970.

The third is from the early 1990s, with the new clock tower, and the street under brick paviours, and where the pedestrian now rules!

ABOVE: *One consistent element in all of the photographs on this page is the overhanging sign of the George & Dragon pub (originally The George commercial hotel). In the days before cars, trains or buses, this is where the stage-coach would set out from for the five hour trip to central London.*

TOP: *The demise of the independent traders. Chesham's celebrations for the 1951 Festival of Britain included a list of the Chamber of Trade and Commerce's town centre retailers under the banner 'Buy Locally and Build Up Chesham's Prosperity'. At the time there were five independent butchers, two fishmongers, eight ladies' outfitters and two tailors for gentlemen, all run by local families.*

Shopping patterns

The town centre street scene has evolved haphazardly, with buildings in a range of styles from various centuries. Each generation of shopkeepers adapted to the demands of consumers, and landlords redeveloped their properties to satisfy the changing needs of retailers. There were few planning regulations enforced to maintain any uniformity of design, or to save buildings of architectural interest. For example, the gabled building to the right of these photographs, occupied by Duce's fish restaurant (later Coral Fish Bar) was of Tudor origin. The Chesham Society campaigned unsuccessfully against its demolition in 1972. Its uncharacterful, box-like replacement can be seen at the top of the opposite page. This was mainly due to the transition during the 1960s from small independent shops to the 'multiples,' as exemplified in the contrast between these two main photographs. The larger, national store names demanded bigger floor spaces and modern fascias. New premises were expanded to the rear and could take deliveries via East Street.

ABOVE & RIGHT: The rise of the retail chains, with multiple locations demanding larger stores, consistent signage and uniform presentation.

ABOVE: The old Woolworth's premises pictured on the opposite page is currently a branch of Costa coffee. With the closure of many pubs, we have now become a nation of coffee drinkers!

BELOW: The High Street has become a place of leisure following pedestrianisation, with outdoor seating, continental style planting and a new cosmopolitan culture.

Chesham is unlike the homogenous modern shopping centre with its ubiquitous shops. It has a range of architecture, some characterful shops and a broad social mix – it is not an elite town, but a healthy blend of people and community activity.

By the end of the 20th century, the shopping habits of the nation had changed radically. Not only had supermarkets dominated the market for groceries, but also out of town retail units and new indoor shopping centres had lured people away from their traditional High Street habitats. The smaller shop premises of Chesham could rarely be adapted to create competitive alternatives and many sat empty and unused. The rise of online shopping is the new threat to the High Street, but our town centre is set to continue its success with a gradual return to traditional values.

We are still blessed with a good range of large chain stores, but the real jewels of Chesham are the independent shops that offer bespoke products, excellent customer service and specialist knowledge. One remarkable example is Darvell's bakery which has traded in Chesham since 1838. Another is Cox the Saddler, selling leather goods since 1911. Turner & Browning opticians has been of service since 1933 and the invaluable Pearces Hardware has been in business since 1938. The trend towards local people setting up unique retail and service outlets of high quality is growing.

The yards

These traditional cobbled lanes were often associated with public houses or light industry, offering a secure place away from the High Street to carry out manual work and to take delivery of goods. Most yards incorporated small workers' cottages, many of which had been declared unfit for habitation by the early 20th century. Chesham lost several of these backwaters to the slum clearances; for example Townfield Yard and Duck Alley – notorious in their time for insanitary living conditions. Their potential for conversion to desirable residences and characterful shops was hidden from those who lacked the necessary vision or foresight to save them. The yards that remain represent an important historical feature of today's town.

RIGHT: These three images of Lum's Yard show the changes to the original picturesque dwellings as they fell into neglect, having been abandoned, and their eventual conversion to boutique-style shops. In the 1980s this renovation project created Darsham Walk – originally a passageway through the heart of the terraced cottages, revealing tiny, low-beamed and somewhat impractical retail spaces, later readjusted to have individual access from the yard and larger, financially viable floor plans.

The photograph *above left* shows the entrance to Lacey's Yard in about 1920. The older buildings here date back to 1649. Several generations of the Lacey family stitched saddles and harnesses within from the late 18th century. Herbert Cox joined them in the 1890s and eventually took over the saddlery business in 1911. His son and grandson succeeded him, and the buildings of Laceys Yard are still owned and cared for by the family. This care is reflected in the attractive shops and garden created by the tenants and enjoyed by the public.

The photograph *above right* shows the entrance to Francis Yard in the 1960s. Clearly, by this time, much of Chesham had become dirty and run down, and it is little wonder that the progressive forces envisaged sweeping away the decaying older premises, to be replaced with clean, ultra-modern shop fronts. Thankfully, the 17th century half-timbered building within Francis Yard has survived intact. During the early 19th century it was the site of The Angel Inn, and Peter Fribbins, a current occupant of Botley House, has discovered a previous name – The King's Head. It was also, quite possibly, the shop of Roger Crab, Chesham's 'mad hatter' and famous English hermit, who lived 1621 to 1680. There is no memorial to him in the town, although long established residents will recall The Mad Hatter café in Red Lion Street.

Currently, Francis Yard is home to Richard Elkington's highly popular Drawingroom art gallery, café and music venue. Remarkably this is not the first music scene to be hosted in Francis Yard. The Trap Door Club at the Botley House stable block saw performances from many renowned folk singers between 1964 and 1967, including Paul Simon and Art Garfunkel. It would be good to see other town yards brought back to life. Tap Yard and Lewins Yard would make prime candidates.

In 1998 Chesham Town Council relocated its Town Hall from the historic Malt House in Elgiva Lane to purpose-built premises in Parsonage Lane at the far end of Star Yard car park, as part of the Sainsbury's redevelopment plans. The entrance to Catling's Garage *(below)* was demolished and a new access from the High Street created with the name Baines Walk, in recognition of the local politician and historian Arnold Baines.

In 1974, Chesham Urban District Council was merged into Chiltern District Council, based in Amersham. Arnold Baines and his fellow councillors fought hard to retain a local Town Council, and won. Without this success, the town could easily have been left without a political voice.

ABOVE: The transformed Lacey's Yard, a centre of wellbeing and creativity; and Francis Yard, home to art, music and alternative living – for which Chesham is gaining a good reputation.

Supermarkets

The first supermarkets appeared in Chesham from the late 1950s. Fine Fare supermarket replaced the Crown Hotel (later becoming Tesco, Bejam, Iceland and others) and Stitcher's supermarket opened to the left of the George & Dragon. Car ownership allowed people to buy in bulk, transporting goods in supermarket trolleys from the stores to large car parks. The days of shoppers walking or cycling with small loads in wicker baskets were numbered. Certainly, the large existing grocers such as the International Stores and the Co-operative outlets were no longer able to offer competitive prices. In 1974, there were reports that the two new supermarkets, Sainsbury's and Waitrose, had resulted in the loss of small, specialist High Street shops. These two supermarkets remain, and although some may consider them as soulless, almost all residents now use them and find their convenience invaluable.

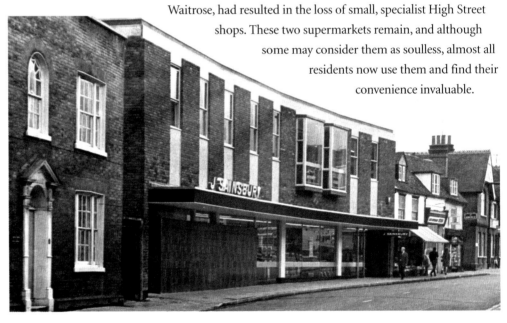

PICTURED: *The House of Tree (the projecting building pictured left and inset) had the last front garden in the High Street. Attempts to put a preservation order on the wisteria creeper at the front failed and it was demolished, to be replaced by the ultra-modern, Brutalist, and highly controversial Waitrose development of 1973. The insensitive design was only slightly softened by using local flints in the concrete façade, but the building is currently well screened with tree planting and is now home to M&Co clothing store, with its spacious, bright, functional interior.*

Upper High Street

This section of the High Street, between the Broadway and Broad Street, was the scene for a major development between the wars for the central store of the Chesham & Wycombe Co-operative Society. This was a fine building with a façade constructed in 1934 from marble, granite, brick and Bath stone. Inside were terrazo floors, oak and walnut panelling, marble shelves and opalite finishings. Tragically, it closed in the 1980s *(pictured above, left)* and was demolished to make way for the Waitrose redevelopment. Although the new supermarket turned its back on the High Street, it did give access via a walkway to The Backs, where the store's car park was sited on the old railway goods yard.

TOP: *An Edwardian view of the Upper High Street. In the distance is the overhanging sign of the Huntsman public house, which was demolished in 1920 prior to the building of the Co-operative premises, now the site of the Waitrose' rear development. The shop of B Stone, Son & Co, joiners, can be seen in the foreground.*

LEFT: *The only consistent part of the built environment in all the main photographs on this page is the three shop premises in the centre of the view. Currently, the interior of one of these terraced cottages has been opened up behind a glass panel to show the original construction.*

A striking difference between such photographs from the 1980s in comparison with those of today (opposite page) is the introduction of trees, planters, street signs and hanging baskets. A more elegant townscape has been created.

BELOW: *Referring to the old view at the top of the page, the joiner's yard is now remembered in the name of the relatively new and attractive Stone's Courtyard.*

Amersham Road

Fitch's service station

BELOW: These photographs show the development of the early fuel facility. Initially a simple layby with petrol pumps, it grew to become the large covered petrol station that we are familiar with today. From the 1920s and until 1937 there was an alternative garage towards Chesham at the Nag's Head, and from 1947 there has been a garage for southbound traffic directly across the road. The large trees have sadly been felled, but the little cottage beyond has remained as the Wheelhouse Veterinary Clinic since 1964.

This book could have opened with a chapter on Amersham Road, as it is one of the earliest recorded new thoroughfares, constructed in 1828, straight up through the woods to Amersham Common. However, this was long before the time of motor cars, and in fact provided an easy run for the timber carters and their horses. For centuries before, they took the old Beech Lane, a meandering route which is still evidenced by a broad ditch running up from Chesham Bois Manor. The road construction was supported by the Cecil family, the Marquesses of Salisbury, who created a route from Hatfield Palace to Salisbury. An old milestone showing distances to Hatfield and Reading can still be found in North Road, Chesham Bois.

Remarkably, the main road is still called 'New Road' by some of Chesham's older residents. An old sign held at Chesham Museum also refers to it as 'Amy Hill'. This is a reference to the mill which stood at the Chesham end. Amy Mill stopped working over a century ago, and the millpond was long used for watercress growing. The mill house, *pictured above left*, stood until 1973, when a lorry crashed there and accelerated its demolition for road widening. It is now the site of the roundabout by Moor Road and Amy Lane, where the attractive Friedrichsdorf Corner has been created to celebrate our German twin town. The Meades Water Gardens were laid out in place of the watercress beds in 1979 and, recently, the Chiltern Chalk Streams Project restored the river bed.

ABOVE: *Mineral Cottage, with its original adjoining wings. It had beautiful rose gardens to the front when this photograph was taken.*

Mineral Cottage

Mineral Cottage was built in 1821 to enclose a chalybeate spring that produced waters rich in iron, reputed to cure many ills. Chesham might have become a prosperous spa town had the spring not failed some years later! During the 20th century, Amersham Road became an increasingly busy thoroughfare and the area around the cottage developed rapidly to serve motor transport at this edge of town location. The Ministry of Housing put the building on its list of special architectural or historic interest in 1969, just as the adjoining land was purchased by a tyre company. The new owners threatened to pull it down in defiance of the preservation order and sparked much local debate. Most residents were happy to accept its demolition and previous owners spoke of the penetrating damp in the walls. However, Val Biro of the Chesham Society considered it a very interesting Regency cottage and we must be grateful for his preservationist mindset. Mineral Cottage still stands and functions well, also serving as a reminder of Chesham's past, in what could otherwise be an unerringly suburban and uninspiring scene. If we allow our passion for car transport and convenience to erase all memories of a slower pace of life, we will be poorer for it.

BELOW: *The site of Amy Mill house prior to the construction of the roundabout at the foot of Amersham Hill. When roads are widened and structured to meet the demands of the national Department for Transport and the local Highways Agency, the impact on the environment ought to be mitigated by tree planting and landscape enhancements.*

Broad Street

The demolition of a public house, The Plough, *pictured above left* at the foot of White Hill, allowed for a large block of flats, shops and an extended petrol filling station in 1960. When St Mary's Way became two-way in 1989, a new roundabout at the junction with Broad Street necessitated the demolition of several shops, shown to the left of the main picture *below*. Before their demise, they had housed memorable businesses such as Don Stevens' cycle shop, Eric the Butcher's, and the Chesham Dairies shop with its milk carton vending machine outside. The Plough filling station, shown *below* with petrol prices from 1984, retained its pump attendants until closure, never moving over to self service. It was eventually replaced by a dry cleaning business.

ABOVE: Formerly known as Hempstead Road, White Hill marked the transition from High Street to Broad Street, and led up to the railway sidings, Chesham Brewery (which closed in 1957) and on to Whitehill School. On the sharp corner of White Hill stood the Three Tuns inn, which closed in 1964 and was taken over by the Council Surveyor's Office. With demolition in 1976, on road safety grounds, it became a car park with large hoardings, and is now a grassy area with a stone martyr's memorial to Thomas Harding.

BELOW RIGHT: St Mary's Way ploughed through the garden of the Waggon & Horses pub, but the Chesham Society had fought hard to retain this building, arguing its importance in closing the view.

The first police station in Broad Street was built in 1861. The large building shown above is the replacement of the 1930s on the same site, known as Copsham House since conversion to offices in the 1990s and then to apartments in 2015. A new police station with limited opening hours remains alongside, but is currently due for closure in 2019, hopefully with a town centre replacement.

PICTURED: *Various traffic calming measures have been implemented over the years along this stretch of road, but there are still issues with air pollution from motor traffic – the days when bicycles outnumbered cars are long gone!*

Flooding has also been a rare but repeated problem over the decades, as the road follows the course of the Vale Brook, a tributary of the River Chess, now only evidenced in a small section of unculverted river in Townsend Road. The planting of trees along this street would be a sensible measure to alleviate issues concerning air quality, flooding and general urban blight.

ABOVE & RIGHT: These three images show the same stretch of road over a period of 100 years. Broad Street was given its name due to the wide thoroughfare created when the old Coughtrey Cottages, which once stood in the middle of the road, were demolished (as pictured). Little else has changed radically, although a notable loss is the elegant iron railings that belonged to the Victorian villas, stripped away for the war effort during the 1940s. Reportedly, very few were ever used for making munitions and ended up being dumped. It would be wonderful if residents could fund their replacement.

BELOW: Pictured is the junction with Townsend Road. This really was the end of town 200 years ago. Early Victorian photographs show a very rural scene, which rapidly became industrialised as Chesham's woodenware, boot and brush factories flourished, and rows of terraced houses were erected to accommodate the workers.

In Townsend Road was Giffard Newton's boot factory (currently occupied by the Workaid charity) and Webb Jarrett's brush factory (which closed in 1982 to become Great Mills DIY store, currently Wickes). Russell's brushmakers still operates in the vicinity.

Berkhampstead Road

Eskdale Avenue, formerly know as Khartoum Road, marks the transition from Broad Street to Berkhampstead Road. For many years, opposite the Jolly Sportsman public house, was Barnes' bakery, later Darvell's *(pictured above and right, top)*. At the top of Eskdale Avenue and White Hill, the Chesham Technical College was established in 1947, later becoming a High School and currently a Grammar School. Another right turn off Berkhampstead Road is Alexander Street *(pictured middle and lower right)*, which in 1971 was widened with the demolition of the New Inn, which had stood at the foot of the street and served local residents and factory workers since 1860.

Berkhampstead Road leads into the heart of Chesham's Newtown, which developed in the late 19th century with the evolution of Chesham's traditional crafts from cottage industries, such as shoe making and wood turning, to factory-based operations focusing on boot making, woodenware manufacture and brush making, along with a wealth of other specialities in the decades that followed (see the book *Chesham at Work in the 20th Century*).

Some housing development east of Berkhampstead Road was delayed due to a long proposed extension of the railway north, but the assault of the motor car came instead, coinciding with the time that south east England was exploding into growth. Britain's first full-length motorway, the M1, opened in 1959 with a junction only 11 miles from Chesham, just beyond Hemel Hempstead.

Pictured below are Nashleigh Garage at the end of Vale Road, now a petrol station, and Chess Medical Centre, opened in 2009 following the demise of Waterside's Cottage Hospital of 1869.

Bellingdon Road

Once a sleepy lane out to the villages, this road has long been a centre of religious worship, beginning with the Quakers, who gathered at their Meeting House at the corner of the road. In 1858, the cemetery, with lodges at each end, was laid out in chalk meadow land that was soon further developed for factories and workers' houses. Townsend Road School *(pictured left, top)* was established nearby in 1874 – now the site of sheltered housing. In the 1920s and '30s one of the first estates of houses was constructed at Pond Park, taking in those people displaced by the slum clearances at Townfield and elsewhere in Chesham. Most of the other housing estates were developed up on the hillsides between 1954 and 1973, with the population of the town growing to over 20,000. Following the electrification of the railway in 1960, Chesham became a commuter town. At the same time, there was a huge influx of new residents, in particular from Harrow and North West London, as well as from Pakistan. In addition to a Methodist church, Bellingdon Road is home to the Chesham Mosque, purpose-built in 2005 *(pictured left, middle)* to replace various temporary premises used since 1970.

A motor garage *(pictured left, bottom)* sits at the end of Bellingdon Road at the fork between Hivings Hill and the Asheridge Road. An industrial estate developed towards Asheridge in the 1950s and remains a thriving centre of business. It stands in stark contrast to the beautiful landscape just beyond it, where Hazeldene Farm invites families to come and see its native rare breed stock. The Chiltern countryside around Chesham is protected by the Metropolitan Green Belt, first enacted in 1938 to prevent London from unchecked growth; also by the Town & Country Planning Act of 1947; and by its designation in 1965 as an Area of Outstanding Natural Beauty.

Waterside

This riverside hamlet has always been a place of industrious endeavour. Four water mills once operated on the length of the river between here and Latimer. Watercress growing and the breeding of Aylesbury ducks also took advantage of the River Chess. There were many cottage industries, such as straw plaiting and lace making.

Between 1949 and 1974, the town's Housing Manager, Mr Saturley, was also the Public Health Inspector. He carried out a vigorous campaign against unfit housing, which brought him into conflict with the defenders of Waterside and the older parts of town, who felt that an opportunity to preserve Chesham's heritage was being lost. Many of the decaying, yet attractive, brick and flint Waterside cottages were demolished, to be replaced with flats, such as those at Riverside Court. However, many older buildings have survived and gone on to be highly valued. They now help maintain the charm of this comparatively rural backwater.

There has remained a great deal of light industry in recent decades, with printing being particularly prevalent in the 1990s. Legislation was enacted in 1973 to banish the juggernauts which were using the Upper Moor as a car park. We must remember that the Moor is common land and belongs to the people. In the 1960s the Lower Moor was used as a rubbish dump by the Urban District Council, helping to level the marshy ground, but leaving some members of the local community to help returf it! Several centres of business have been transformed – for example Chiltern House on the site of Shackman's, the prestigious jewellers old premises, and latterly The Bagnall Centre for Integrative Healthcare in the old Hayes boot factory. In 1995, a series of events to celebrate Waterside's industries were organised between Waterside School and Christ Church.

ABOVE: *The 30-foot overshot wheel at the rear of Lord's Mill was damaged by an earth tremor and replaced by a smaller interior wheel, powered by steam, in 1900.*

Lord's Mill

Lord's Mill was constructed about 1660. Its solid oak structure was reportedly still as hard as rock three hundred years later in the 1960s. This is the site of Chesham's mill mentioned in the Domesday book. Its one thousand year old millpond was most likely created under the instruction of Lady Elgiva, wife of Saxon King Edwy. In the 10th century the river was diverted from its natural course (now the curve of Moor Road) in order to build a head of water.

After centuries of milling by water power, it eventually converted to steam, as the flow of the river had diminished, and finally to electric. Flour milling ended in the 1920s, but the Wright family continued to use the mill for other purposes, including the preparation of animal feeds. When ill health forced them to close the business in 1973, their initial intention was to convert the mill to accommodation. In that same year, Colin Amery, features editor of *The Architects Journal*, described the building as 'a great treasure'. In 1978 it was sold to a sheet metal company, and ten years after that it was demolished. Councillor Arnold Baines described the decision as 'a barberous act of vandalism.'

RIGHT: *Lord's Mill under demolition in 1988. The authorities had seemingly blocked all attempts to convert the decaying building to a home, craft centre or museum. Bucks County Council Highways Department reportedly wanted the mill removed as part of their road improvement plans.*

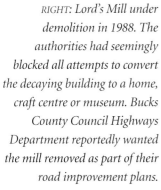

RIGHT & ABOVE: *Today the fine old millhouse remains. Perhaps a mill wheel could one day be re-installed on site, similar to this one photographed in 1959, probably from Canon's Mill, further downstream.*

Bridges

PICTURED: *In 1887, the people of Chesham campaigned to get their railway station in the heart of the town, rather than the proposed terminus on the Moor. Their success two years later necessitated construction of two bridges, one by the New Inn in Waterside and one in Moor Road. The New Inn came down in 1971, but the bridges lasted until 1986, when they were due for replacement. The local branch line of the London Transport rail service was threatened with closure as a result, but thankfully funding for two new bridges was found. Pictured crossing the Moor Road bridge is the last of the steam trains (left) and the new electric rail stock of 1960 (below left).*

BELOW LEFT: *China Bridge was a wooden structure that crossed over to Shantung Place, the terrace of houses on Moor Road. The well constructed Kitty's Bridge still stands a little up-river.*

BELOW RIGHT: *Steps lead up over the stream to today's Chesham Moor Gym & Swim, a wonderful amenity for the town, with its long-established outdoor pool.*

Community venues

Creating and retaining good community facilities relies on the power of local authorities, the goodwill of successful businesses and the cohesion of the community itself. Here are some fine local examples.

In 1967, Whitehill school closed down. It had served boys, girls and infants since 1891, but the expanding population had gradually made its facilities redundant. The infants moved to Newtown School in the 1930s. The boys moved to Thomas Harding in 1966 and in the following year the girls were transferred to Brushwood. The school sat empty until it returned to use as a Teachers' Centre in 1970. That same year, Chesham hosted a Millenary Festival to celebrate the town's recorded history. Cic Upcott, *pictured above*, volunteered to bring the exhibition up to date with a display of local arts and crafts at the old school in White Hill. It was such a success that it bonded the community, which fought for the retention of the building as a local asset when the County Council planned to sell it in 1974. The Chesham & District Community Association was formed, and from 1976 it established the White Hill Centre, which still functions today as a venue for arts, crafts, education, sports and leisure.

In 1977, a Chesham businessman and self-made millionaire, Douglas McMinn, created a day centre for the elderly in East Street. The McMinn Centre, a wonderful symbol of philanthropy, was officially opened by a less celebrated figure, Jimmy Saville, in 1979! Sadly it closed in 2015.

In 1998 the new Elgiva was constructed as a purpose-built theatre and cinema at Albany Place, off St Mary's Way, and was officially opened by entertainer Danny LaRue. It had been part of the Sainsbury's redevelopment and relied heavily on funding from this large corporate company. The legacy of the previous Elgiva venue was hard to dispel, but under the current management of Mark Barnes and his team it has become a financially sustainable and much valued community arts venue owned by Chesham Town Council.